Lake Country School
Montessori Learning Environments
3755 Pleasant Av. S.
Minneapolis, MN 55409

MINNESOTA IN MAPS: A TRAILBLAZER ATLAS*

By Constance Jefferson Sansome, Ph.D.

Illustrations by Constance J. Sansome and Lisa E. Jefferson

***Trailblazer Books** — helping children and adults explore, appreciate, and understand Minnesota's natural heritage.

Dedication: For Nick and Dain, Crystal and Sierra, and all young people curious about the world they live in.

Acknowledgements: Many thanks to Kathy and Steve Albers, Marlys Ayotte, Gayle Collins, Tom Cousins, Ellen Cox, Rick Dahlman, Michelle DeLorme, Corrine Dwyer, B.J. Farley, David Grigal, Dave Hagen, Barbara Hill, Mike Hoffman, Tim Jefferson, Tom Lebovsky, Mary Moch, Howard Moehrs, Northfield sixth graders, Frank Pinokey, Michelle Potter, D. Rademacher, St. Paul Chamber of Commerce, Lois Stanfield, Ahava Silkey, Gloria Warnholtz, Bruce Watson, Mark Witt, and Joy Wolf. Special thanks to Pat Bell, Gary DeGrote, Karen Elmers, Margery Facklam, Sybil Smith, the Northfield Writer's Group, Ken Sansome, and Joan Wolf. You have all contributed to the success of this project.

Book Design: C.J. Sansome

Copyright© 1990 Constance J. Sansome
All Rights Reserved

No part of this book may be reproduced or transmitted in any form or by any means electronic or mechanical, including photocopying, recordings, or by an information storage and retrieval system, except for brief quotations embodied in critical essays and reviews, without prior written permission from the publisher.

Published by Trailblazer Books
13030 Cannon City Blvd.
Northfield, Minnesota 55057
(507) 645-4242

Trade Distribution by Voyageur Press
Box 338, 123 North Second Street
Stillwater, Minnesota 55082
(612) 430-2210, (800) 888-9653

Printed in the United States of America   Northfield Printing, Inc. Northfield, Minnesota 55057
ISBN 0-9626025-0-7 (hardcover)   2 3 4 5   **ISBN 0-9626025-1-5** (softcover)   2 3 4 5

Minnesota in Maps: A Trailblazer Atlas

Contents

Minnesota and the World (Chapter 1) 4-5

Lakes, Rivers, and Streams (Chapter 2) 6-7

Hills, Plains, and Valleys (Chapter 3) 8-9

Rocks (Chapter 4) 10-11

Climate (Chapter 5) 12-13

Soils (Chapter 6) 14-15

Plant Life (Chapter 7) 16-17

Animal Life (Chapter 8) 18-19

People, Cities, and Highways (Chapter 9) 20-21

People at Work (Chapter 10) 22-23

People at Play (Chapter 11) 24-25

More Maps (Chapter 12) 26-27

If You Want to Know More 28-29
    Cited References; Suggestions for Further Reading; Places to Visit
    Activities and Questions; Miscellaneous Facts and Figures

Glossary 30

Index 31-32

Minnesota and the World

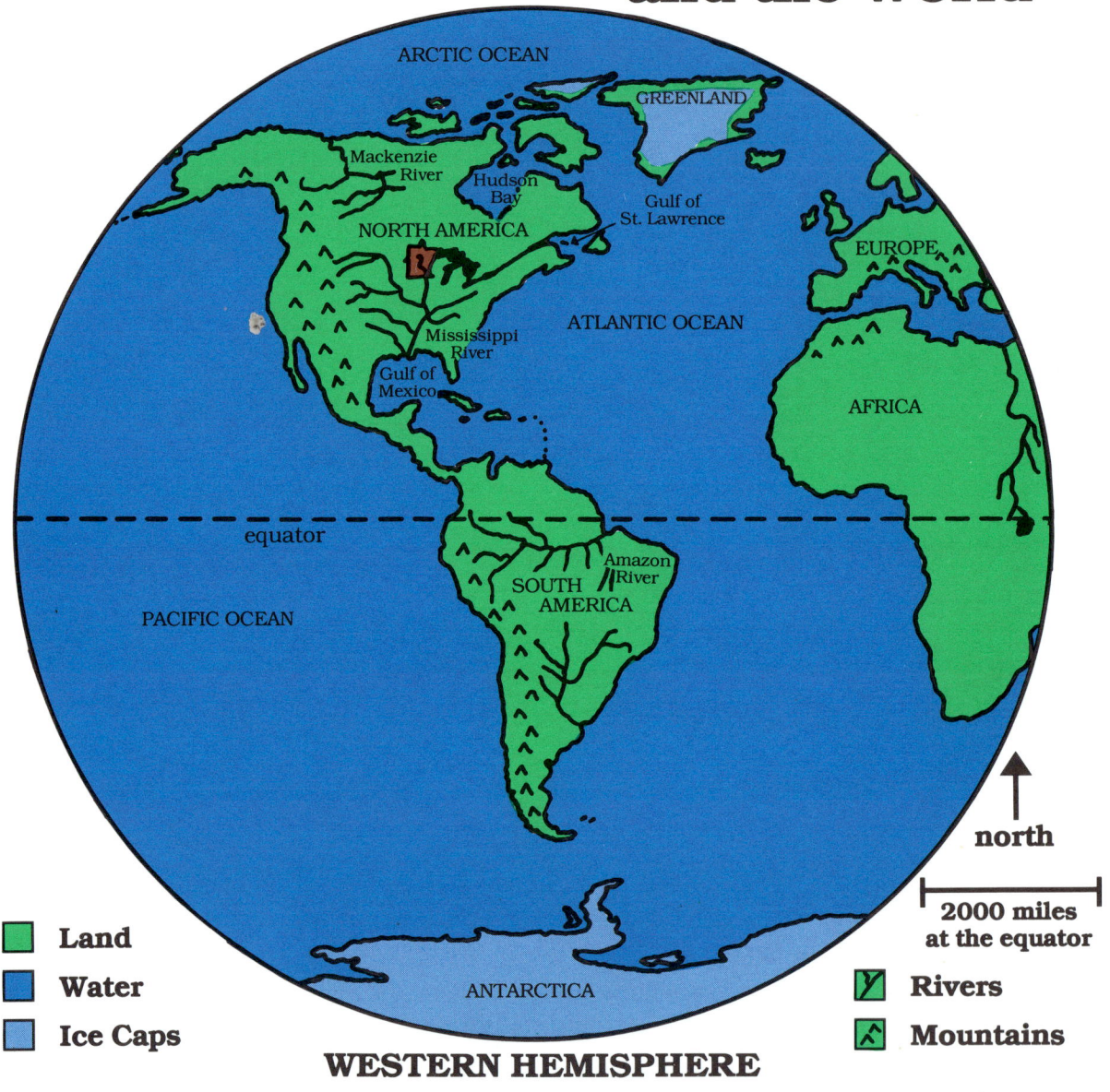

WESTERN HEMISPHERE

World Comparisons:	🚩 Minnesota:	● The Earth:
total surface area (square miles)	84,068	196,940,400
water area (square miles)	4,779	139,090,400
highest/lowest points (feet, on land)	2,301/602	29,029/−1,312
highest/lowest temperatures (degrees °F)	114/−59	136/−129
greatest/least rainfall (inches per year)	52/8	>600/<1
total population (year of estimate)	4,306,550 (1988)	5,192,000,000 (1989)
largest metropolitan area (1988)	Minneapolis-St. Paul 2,182,181	Tokyo 27,700,000

Chapter 1

Minnesota and the World

Minnesota — there's magic in the name: ten thousand lakes, towering white pines, showy ladyslippers, northern pike, timber wolves; also prairies, forests and wetlands; dairy cattle and iron mines.

Minnesota is located approximately halfway between the Pacific and Atlantic oceans, Hudson Bay and the Gulf of Mexico, and absolutely halfway between the equator and north pole.

"Minnesota" is an Indian word meaning "land of sky-tinted waters." The state is the birthplace of the Mississippi River, "The Father of Waters," and bordered by Lake Superior, "The Big-Sea-Shining-Water." Minnesota is pockmarked and cut by seemingly uncountable other lakes, rivers, streams, ponds, and marshes. The state has hills and plains, valleys and ridges and hollows. Its landscape is the gift of glaciers.

Minnesota has short hot summers and long cold winters. Its soils are among the world's richest; its rocks some of the world's most ancient. Oaks, maples, and spruce; corn, soybeans, and sugar beets grow here.

Minnesotans — there are approximately four million of these people, a very small portion of the world's five billion people. Minnesotans are farmers and foresters, miners, manufacturers, tradespeople, financiers and educators. They are people of predominately German and Scandinavian heritage, Protestant and Catholic faith. Minnesotans are vigorous, long-lived outdoor people who ski, skate, sail, swim, hike, camp, and fish.

Minnesota covers only 84,000 square miles of the earth's 197,000,000 square miles. But it is large enough, diverse enough, to live in and explore for a lifetime.

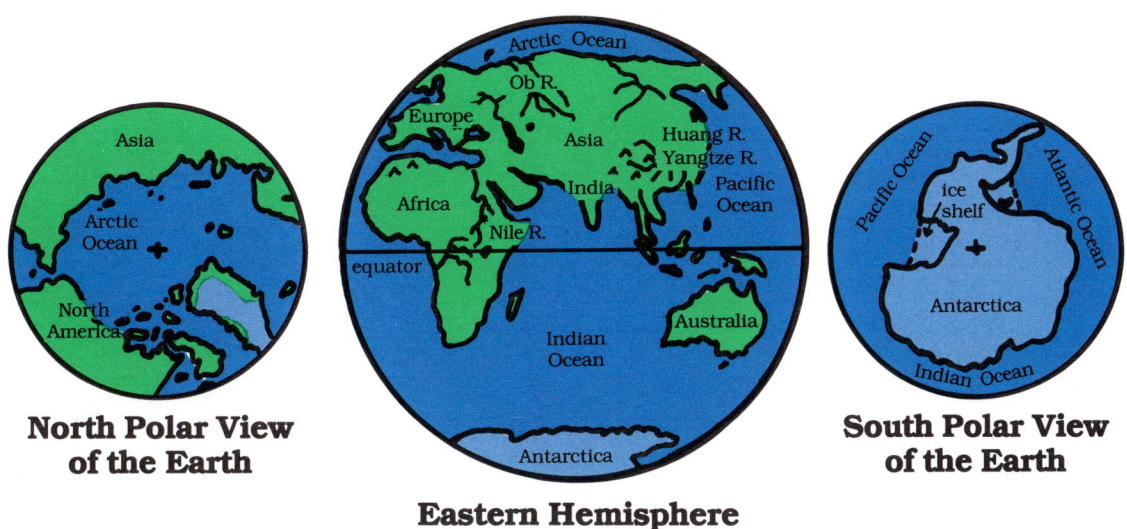

North Polar View of the Earth

Eastern Hemisphere

South Polar View of the Earth

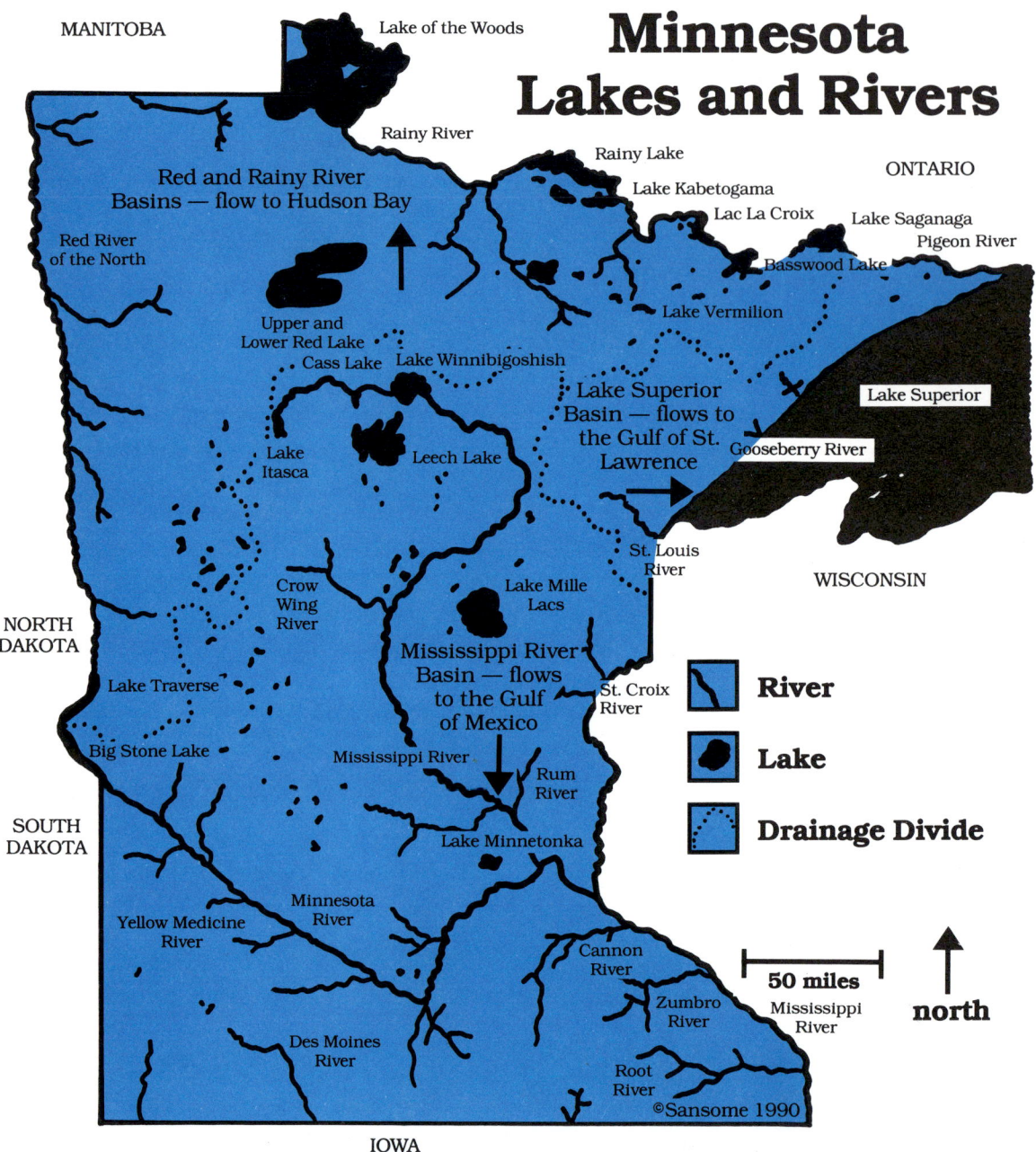

Minnesota Lakes and Rivers

The World's Six Longest Rivers

Name	Continent	Length (miles)
Nile	Africa	4,145
Amazon	S. America	4,000
Yangtze	Asia	3,900
Mississippi	N. America	3,740
Huang	Asia	3,395
Ob	Asia	3,362

data from *Goode's World Atlas*, 18th Ed.

Minnesota's Six Largest Lakes
(those entirely within the state)

Name	Size (acres)	Miles of Shoreline	Max Depth (feet)
Red	275,000	*123	35
Mille Lacs	132,516	86	35
Leech	111,527	190	150
Winnibigoshish	53,544	*116	70
Vermilion	40,557	*186	76
Cass	15,596	*41	120

data from the MDNR, 1990; * Grossman and Thomsen, 1987

Chapter 2

Lakes, Rivers, and Streams

Minnesota is called the "Land of 10,000 Lakes." This nickname once appeared on every license plate. Actually the state has thousands more — 15,291 lakes each covering ten acres or more. Some lakes are big, others small; some deep, others shallow; some are rounded, others irregular; some clear and others murky. Between, connecting, and draining the lakes are thousands of winding rivers and streams. Minnesota is the source of the Mississippi, the world's fourth longest river, and borders Lake Superior, the world's largest freshwater lake. The state has more shoreline than California and Oregon combined.

Lake Superior splashes against Minnesota's rocky North Shore. Strung along Minnesota's northern border are other large lakes — Lake of the Woods, Rainy, Kabetogama, La Croix, Basswood, and Saganaga. Farther south are Upper and Lower Red, Vermilion, Winnebigoshish, Leech, Mille Lacs, and Minnetonka. Not shown on your map are thousands of other lakes, dozens of them named Round or Long or Big; others with Indian names such as Minnewaska, Ogiskemuncie, and Pokegama; many with bird or animal names such as Eagle, Loon, Bear, Moose, and Otter. Many Minnesota lakes have formed in hollows left by glaciers; others have formed behind levees and dams built by rivers, beavers, and man.

Minnesota waters flow in three directions. The Mississippi and its tributaries, of central and southern Minnesota — including the Crow Wing and Rum, Yellow Medicine and Minnesota, St. Croix, Zumbro, Root, and Des Moines — flow south to the Gulf of Mexico. The Red and Rainy rivers of western and northern Minnesota flow north through Lake Winnipeg to Hudson Bay and the Arctic Ocean. Minnesota's North Shore rivers — including the Pigeon, Gooseberry, and St. Louis — flow east through the Great Lakes and St. Lawrence River to the North Atlantic. Minnesota's thousands of other rivers and streams, named and unnamed, follow these three major drainages to the sea.

Minnesota lakes, rivers, and streams provide homes for waterlilies, crayfish, crappies, and clams. They are the feeding ground for heron, raccoon, and otter. They serve as drinking fountain, highway, playground, sewer, and power source for man.

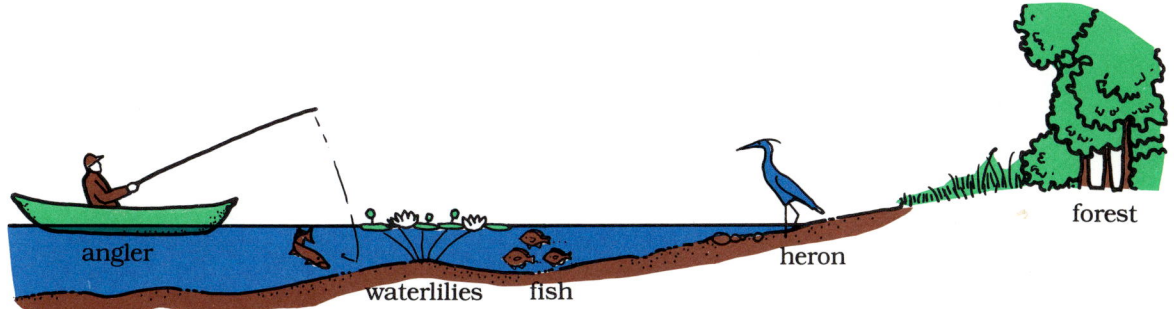

Lake Cross-Section

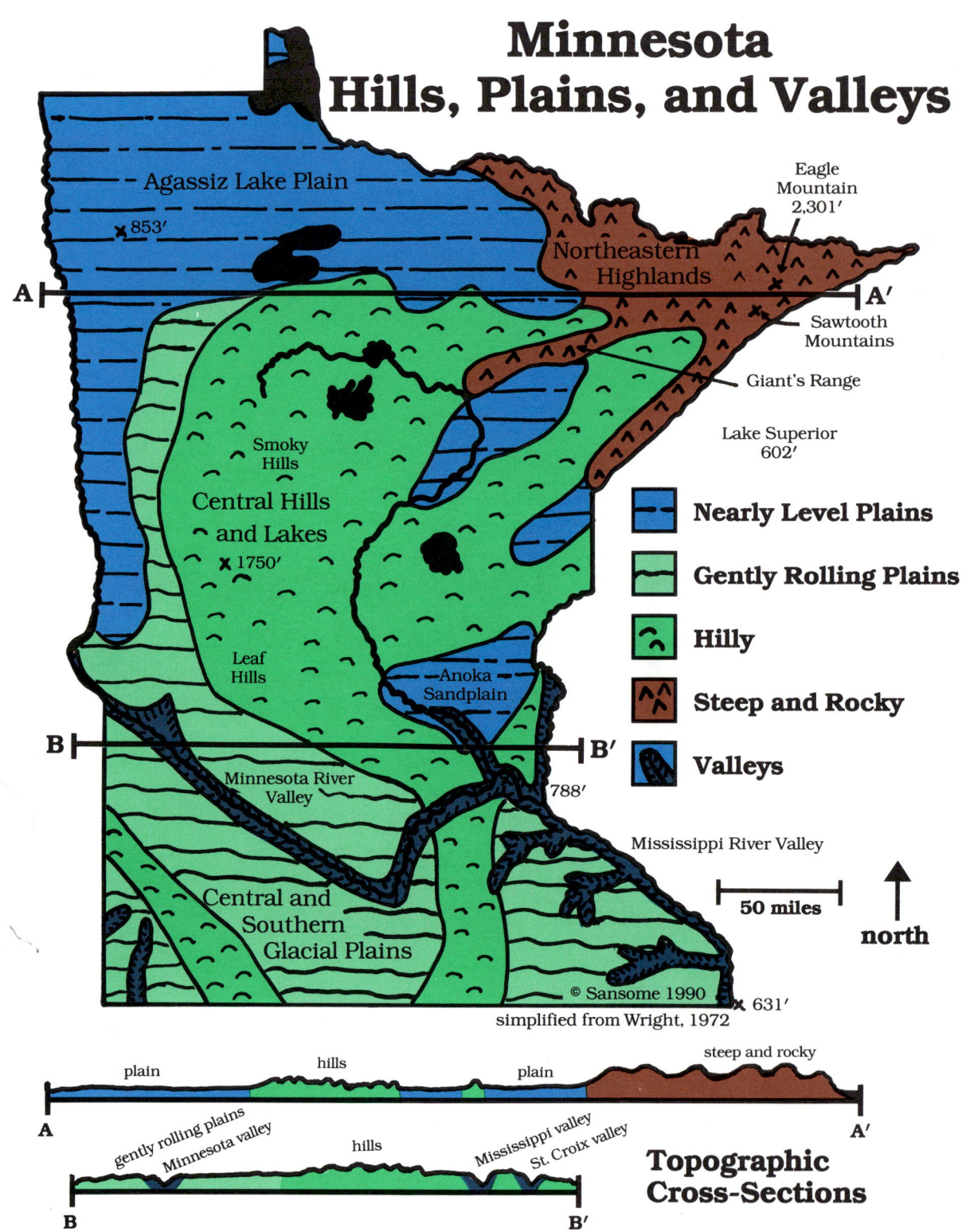

Chapter 3

Hills, Plains, and Valleys

Minnesota is a land of hills, plains, valleys, and worn-down mountains — the Leaf Hills and Smoky Hills, the Agassiz Lake Plain and Anoka Sandplain, the Minnesota and Mississippi and St. Croix valleys, the Sawtooth Mountains and the Giant's Range among others. The top of Eagle Mountain, at 2,301 feet above sea level, is the highest point in the state. The shore of Lake Superior, at 602 feet above sea level, is the lowest.

Northeastern Minnesota is the most rugged part of the state. Here high rock ridges and knobs separate deep rock-bound lakes. In southeastern Minnesota, nearly level uplands are cut by steep-sided valleys. Bluffs rise 400-500 feet above the Mississippi and its tributary streams. Central Minnesota is crowded with small hills and dotted with numerous lakes. Local relief, the difference between the high and low points of the landscape, is often 200-300 feet. Southwestern Minnesota is gently rolling with broad shallow lakes. Northwestern Minnesota is almost flat, its local relief less than five feet.

Minnesota's landscapes are the gift of glaciers, huge masses of ice which crept across the state several times during the past two million years. These glaciers, often a mile thick, gouged out dirt and rock to make the ridges, knobs, and lake basins of the northeast. They carried that rock debris southward and, on melting, dropped it in the irregular hills and hollows of the central part of the state and the long rolling plains of the southwest. Huge rivers of glacial meltwater cut the deep valleys of southeastern Minnesota.

As the glaciers melted into northwestern Minnesota, they blocked the natural drainage to Hudson Bay. An immense lake, Glacial Lake Agassiz, formed behind the ice. This lake eventually spread across northwestern Minnesota and adjacent parts of the Dakotas and Canada. When the last ice melted, approximately 9,000 years ago, the waters drained away leaving behind vast stretches of flat prairie and swampland known as the Agassiz Plain.

Minnesotans use their hilly, irregular land for recreation and pasture. They use their flat and gently sloping lands for farms, highways, and towns.

rolling hills and kettle lakes
of central Minnesota

Sawtooth Mountains
of northeastern Minnesota

Agassiz Lake Plain of northwestern Minnesota.
Much of this is also known as the Red River Valley.

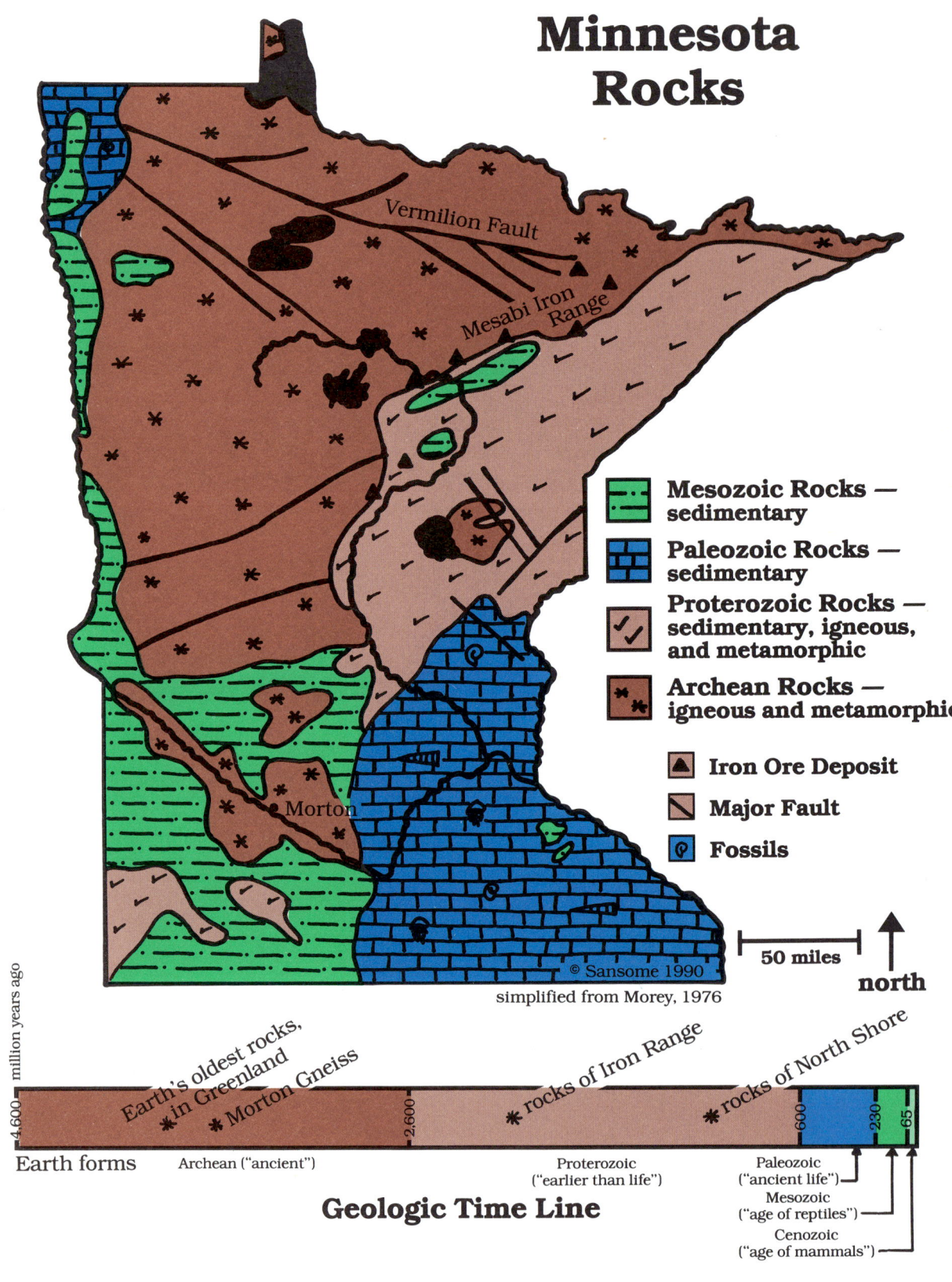

Chapter 4

Rocks

Minnesota has rocks that were once the mud of warm shallow seas, others the steaming lava pouring from volcanic vents, and yet others the shifting sands of an ancient beach. Some of these rocks formed when only microscopic life was present on earth, others when cephalopods, huge squid-like animals, ruled the seas, and still others formed when dinosaurs roamed the lands.

A swirled and banded rock, pink, gray, and black, is found in the Minnesota River Valley near the town of Morton. This, the Morton Gneiss, is the world's second oldest known rock. It formed 3.6 billion years ago when the earth's surface was still warm and mobile.

Red, yellow, and black iron-rich rocks, found on the Minnesota iron ranges, are approximately two billion years old. They contain traces of primitive microorganisms which manufactured food from sunlight, water, and carbon dioxide. Dark gray basalts and bright sparkling granites, found along the North Shore and Canadian Border, formed during times of volcanism and mountain uplift one billion and more years ago.

Shales, sandstones, and limestones are found throughout southeastern Minnesota. These rocks, rich in fossil shells, record the life and movements of warm shallow seas which moved back and forth across North America between 350 and 600 million years ago. Whitish clays found in western Minnesota indicate a hot, wet climate during the Age of Dinosaurs, approximately 100 million years ago.

Great fractures, or faults, cut across the rocks of northern and central Minnesota. These fractures mark ancient breaks and shifts in the earth's crust. One of these faults, the Vermilion, runs for hundreds of miles across northern Minnesota. It is as large as the great faults of Canada, Scotland, and California.

People use Minnesota's rocks for building stone and road gravel. They use the iron for making steel, the quartz for glass, and the clay for tiles. Geologists continually examine the rocks for new and increasingly valuable deposits of oil, cobalt, platinum, titanium, diamonds, zinc, manganese, silver, and gold.

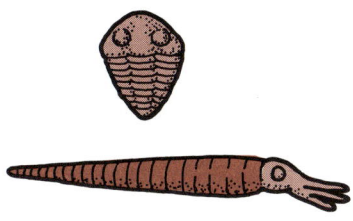

fossil animals

close-up of
Morton Gneiss

geologist examining
rock outcrop

World Climates

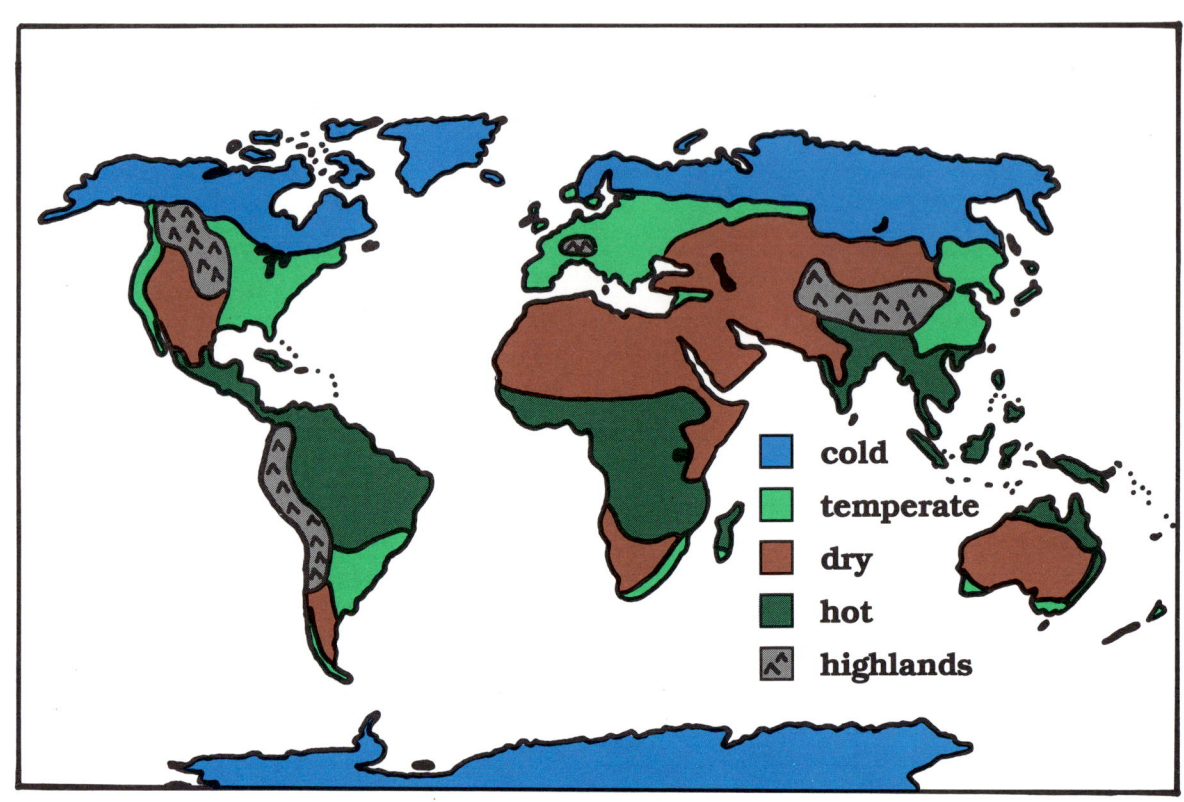

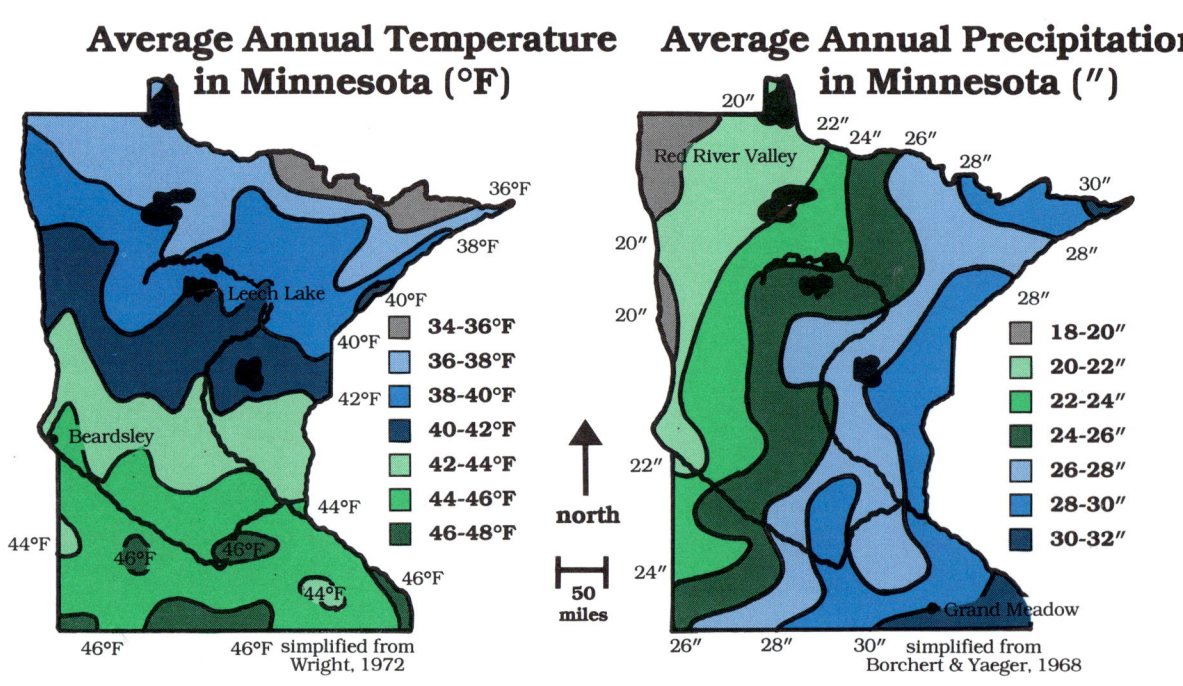

Chapter 5

Climate

Sun and rain, heat and cold, pounding hail, silent snow, tornado. Soft April mornings. Crisp October afternoons. Minnesota has weather for watching and walking, skiing and skating, swimming and sunbathing. It has weather for the June bug and cicada, the snowshoe hare and the snowy owl. Minnesota weather changes by the season, the day, and often the hour. Weather averaged over a long period of time is called climate.

Minnesota, far from the moderating effect of oceans and halfway between the equator and the pole, has a climate of extremes. Summers are short, sticky, and hot with temperatures often climbing into the 90's. Winters are long, dry, and very cold with temperatures often falling to 30 below zero. In July, at Beardsley, the temperature once hit 114 degrees Fahrenheit. In February, near Leech Lake, the temperature once hit 59 below.

Precipitation? Rain and snow, hail and sleet all fall on Minnesota — 20 to 30 inches each year, with the least falling in the northwest and the most in the southeast. In 1936 less than eight inches of precipitation fell in the Red River Valley. In 1911 more than 51 inches was recorded at Grand Meadow. Snow can fall on Halloween. Rain can fall on Christmas. In the Twin Cities snowmen can last from Thanksgiving to Easter.

Storms? Minnesota has plenty. Thunderstorms with heavy rains, high winds, lightning, and sometimes hail occur in summer. Tornadoes are feared spring and early summer invaders. They are the earth's most powerful and erratic storms. They spin like tops, pack winds to 400 miles per hour, roar like locomotives, uproot trees, and blow down buildings. Blizzards are dangerous winter storms of heavy snow, piercing winds, and rapidly falling temperatures.

Yet Minnesotans, with their warm strong buildings and steep roofs built to keep out the cold and wind and shed the rain and snow, like their weather. They talk of it constantly, forecasting the corn harvest or predicting the sailing winds. They say that their climate is invigorating, keeps them hardy, and builds their character. Minnesotans thoroughly enjoy their warm spring mornings, long cool summer evenings, hazy autumn days, and brilliant winter nights.

Minnesota Frost-Free Season
1. less than 100 days
2. 100-120 days
3. 120-140 days
4. 140-160 days
5. more than 160 days

after Borchert and Gustafson, 1980

children playing in the snow

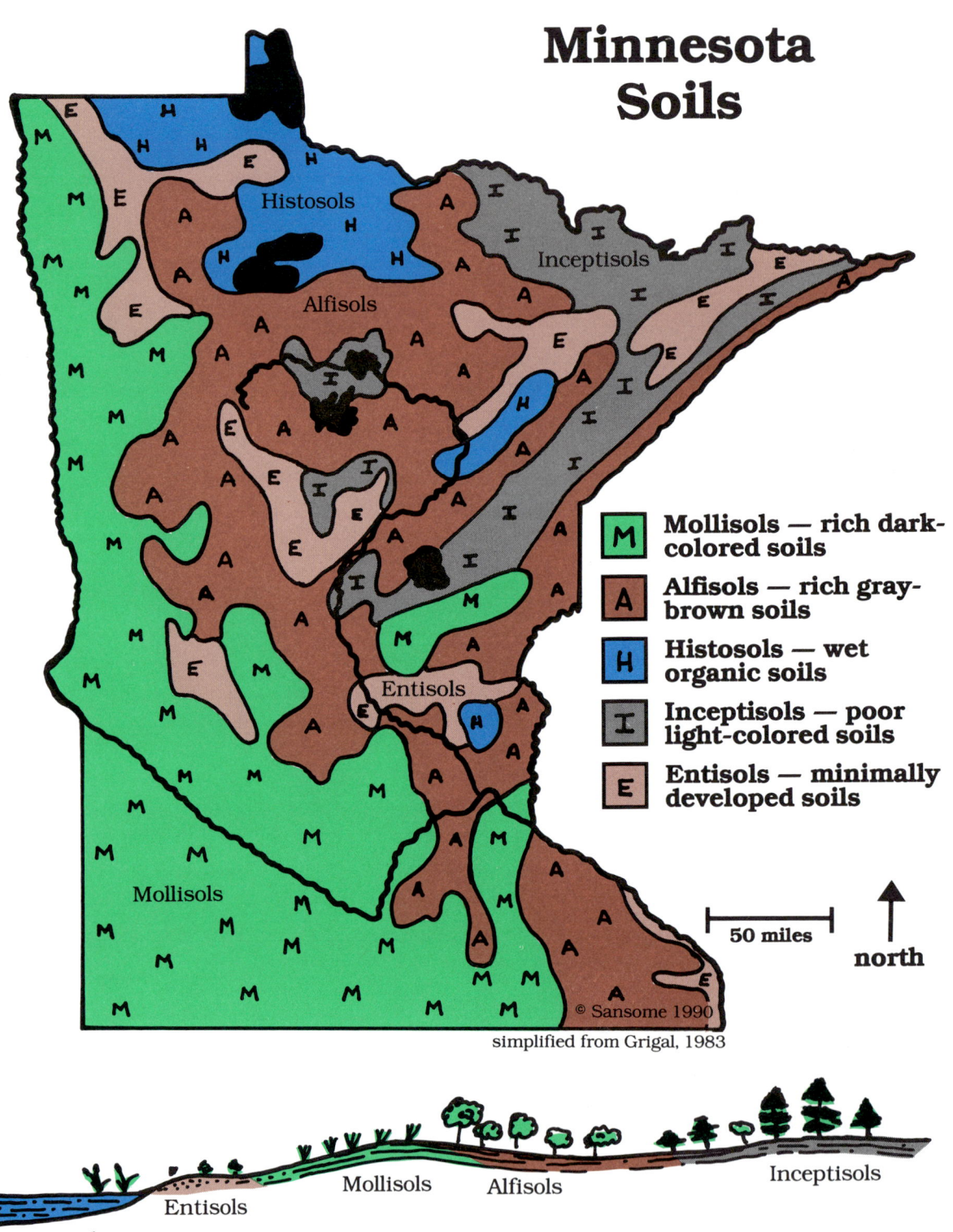

Chapter 6

Soils

Soils are one of man's most important natural resources. Soils are necessary for the growth of green plants, the food of animals. Soils may be wet or dry, fine or coarse, hard or soft. They are made of minerals, plant and animal remains, water, and air.

Soil type and thickness depends on climate and relief, underlying rock material, plant and animal life, and time. Minnesota soils have developed under grass and forest, in swamps and bogs, on hilltops and hillsides, and in valleys. They have formed on sand and gravel, clay and silt and solid rock. Most have developed since glaciation, during the past 10,000 years.

Some of the world's best farming soils occur in southern and western Minnesota. These thick, dark, and nutrient-rich soils are called Mollisols. They formed under prairie grass. Similar soils are found in Uruguay, Paraguay, and the Russian Ukraine. Mollisols are excellent for corn, soybeans, wheat, tomatoes, and squash. Rich gray-brown soils are found in central Minnesota. These soils, called Alfisols, formed under hardwood forest. Similar soils cover much of the Midwest and Europe. Alfisols are good for corn, hay, and pasture.

Nutrient-poor, light-colored soils are spread across northeastern Minnesota, much of southern Canada, and northern Asia. These soils, formed in a cold climate under mixed conifer-deciduous forest, are called Inceptisols. They have been used for growing rutabagas. Wet soils composed of decaying plants are found in Minnesota swamps, marshes, and bogs. These soils are called Histosols. They are used for growing wild rice, willow, and cranberry. Entisols, shallow minimally developed soils, occur on sand, rock, and young water-deposited materials. Pine, aspen, and cottonwood grow on them.

Soils are slow to form and easy to destroy. They are easily blown away and washed away. They can be compacted, moved around, and worn out. Minnesotans try hard to conserve their soil with windbreaks, check dams, contour farming, minimal tillage, and fertilizer.

farmer disking and fertilizing field

plants

topsoil —
rich in organic matter:
plants, fungi, bacteria, insects

subsoil —
rich in minerals,
especially clay; includes
pieces of parent material

parent material —
glacial debris, rock,
or other material

Soil Profile

Minnesota Native Plant Life

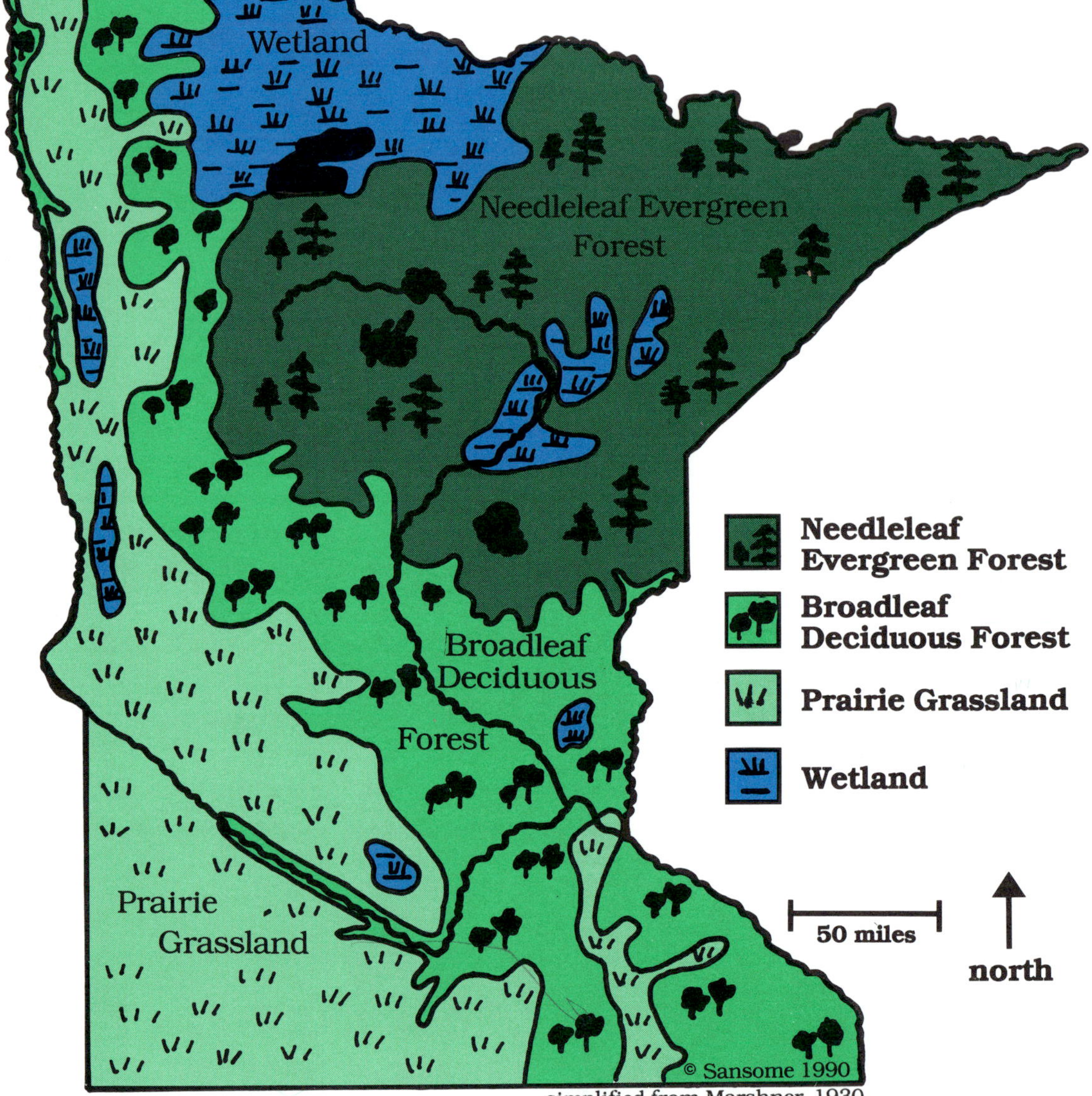

Legend:
- Needleleaf Evergreen Forest
- Broadleaf Deciduous Forest
- Prairie Grassland
- Wetland

50 miles

north

© Sansome 1990
simplified from Marshner, 1930

North America — Native Plant Life

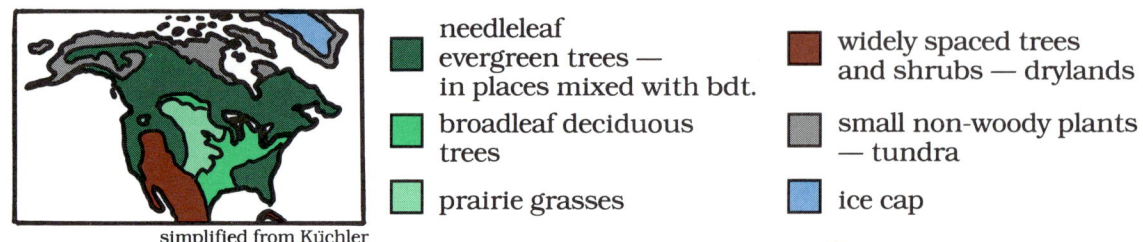

- needleleaf evergreen trees — in places mixed with bdt.
- broadleaf deciduous trees
- prairie grasses
- widely spaced trees and shrubs — drylands
- small non-woody plants — tundra
- ice cap

simplified from Küchler

Chapter 7

Plant Life

Minnesota lies at the intersection of North America's western prairie, northern evergreen forest, and eastern deciduous forest. Here waving grass meets spreading oak and towering pine.

Prairie grows in the warm and dry, southern and western parts of the state. Broken now by plow and fence, it once extended from Ohio to the Rocky Mountains and from the Mackenzie River to northern Mexico. To the pioneers it seemed an endless sea of grass edged only by sky. In places the big bluestem and Indian grass, butterfly weed, blazing star, and goldenrod grew dense and tall enough to hide buffalo, people, and horses.

Evergreen forest, dark, often impenetrable and mysterious, grows in Minnesota's cool and moist northeast. It spreads from there far into the wild lands north and east of Lake Superior, then on across eastern Canada to the Gulf of St. Lawrence. Its needleleaf, cone-bearing, always green pines, spruces, and firs are often known as "Christmas trees."

Deciduous forest, characterized by broad-leaved trees which lose their leaves in winter, grows in eastern and southeastern Minnesota. It occupies a narrow band between the grasses and evergreens. This woods of elm and oak, maple and hickory, runs eastward to the Atlantic coast.

In some places prairie and deciduous forest grade into one another — oaks thrive amongst grasses. In other places the evergreen and deciduous forest intermingle — birch and aspen appear with pine and spruce.

In wet places, scattered throughout the state, grow moisture-loving plants such as cattail and tamarack, willow, sedge, and moss. In some northern wetlands grow the insect-eating pitcher plant and sundew.

When settlers first came to Minnesota, prairie, forest, and wetland covered the state. But little of this native vegetation remains. Prairie has been plowed under for corn, forest cut over for lumber, and wetland drained for agriculture and housing. Minnesotans, however, are beginning to realize that the world is not nearly so beautiful or diverse without its native plant life. They are attempting to preserve selected natural areas and restore others.

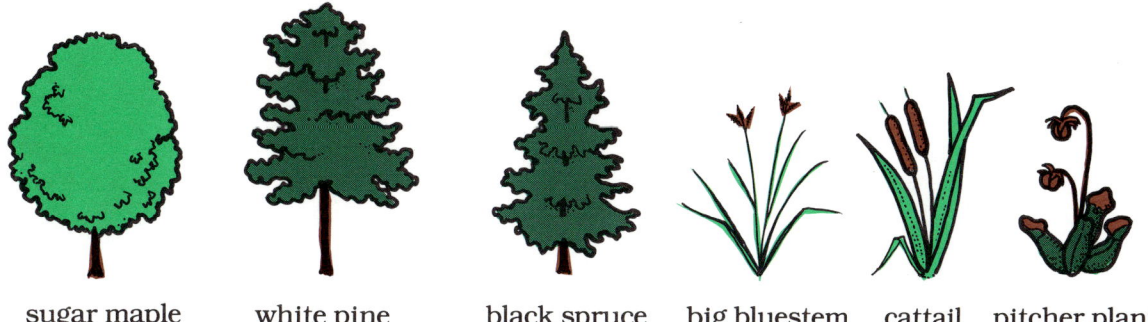

sugar maple   white pine   black spruce   big bluestem   cattail   pitcher plant

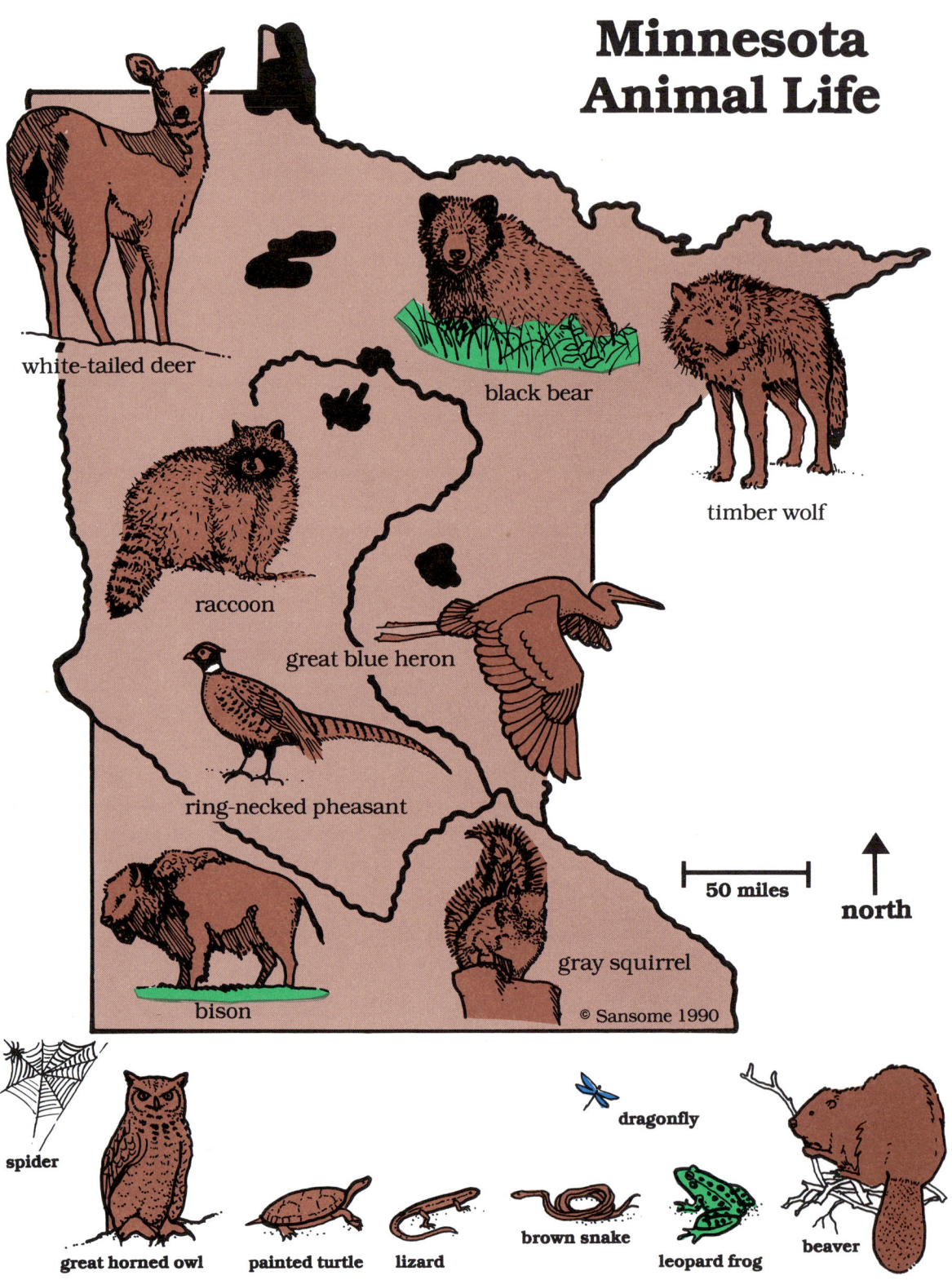

Chapter 8

Animal Life

Minnesota has timber wolves and black bears, bald eagles and blue herons, milk snakes, snapping turtles, and walleyed pike. It has garden spiders, dragonflies, millipedes, mosquitoes, and earthworms. Minnesota's animal life is abundant and diverse because of the state's varied topography, climate, soils, and vegetation.

There are 80 species of mammals, 220 birds, 27 reptiles, 18 amphibians, and 144 species of fish living in the state. The mammals, ranging from the tiny one-ounce pigmy shrew to the half-ton moose, include opossums, moles, bats, rabbits, woodchucks, squirrels, gophers, porcupines, raccoons, weasels, otters, skunks, foxes, lynx, and elk.

The reptile species include three lizards, nine turtles, and 16 snakes. Only the rattlesnakes, found in southeastern Minnesota, are poisonous. The amphibians include the tiger salamander, common toad, leopard frog, and four different tree frogs.

Minnesota birds include the gray jay which prefers the conifer forest, the cardinal which prefers the deciduous forest, the meadowlark which inhabits the prairie, and the red-winged blackbird which inhabits the marsh. Ruffed grouse live in the northern forest. Ring-necked pheasants, introduced to the state in 1905, live in the farmlands.

Minnesota's fish, abundant in most lakes and streams, include sunfish, crappies, perch, bullheads, bass, trout, and pike. The largest fish ever caught was a 92-pound sturgeon.

During the past 130 years, people have greatly changed the state's natural habitats. They have cultivated the prairie, cut the forest, drained the wetlands, channeled the streams, dammed the rivers, and hunted to excess. They have eliminated a few animal species, reduced the numbers of others, and changed the distribution of many.

Woodland caribou and passenger pigeons are extinct. Peregrine falcons, burrowing owls, trumpeter swans, and whooping cranes are endangered. Black bear and timber wolf, once widespread, are confined to Minnesota's wooded northeast. White-tailed deer have spread from southern Minnesota into the cutover forest lands of the north. Franklin's ground squirrel has moved from the prairie into farmyards, dumps, and state parks.

simplified from Borchert and Yaeger, 1986

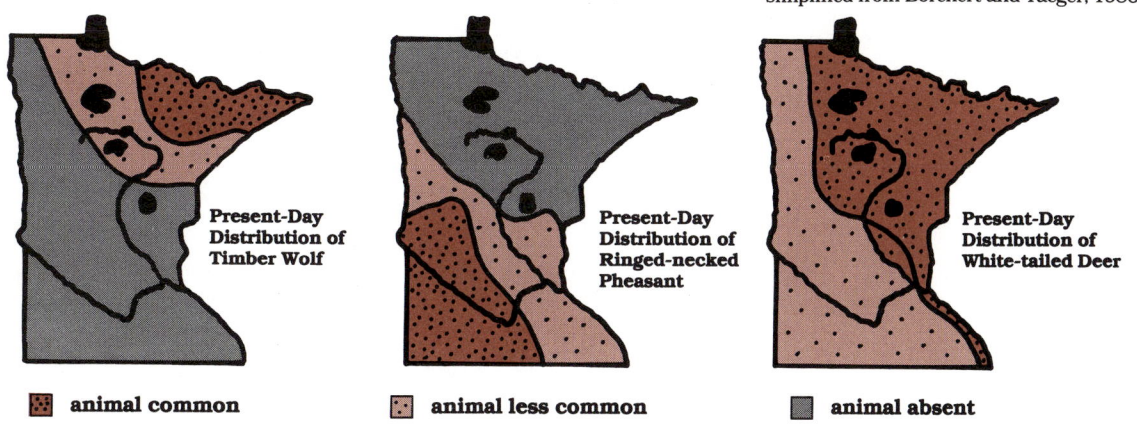

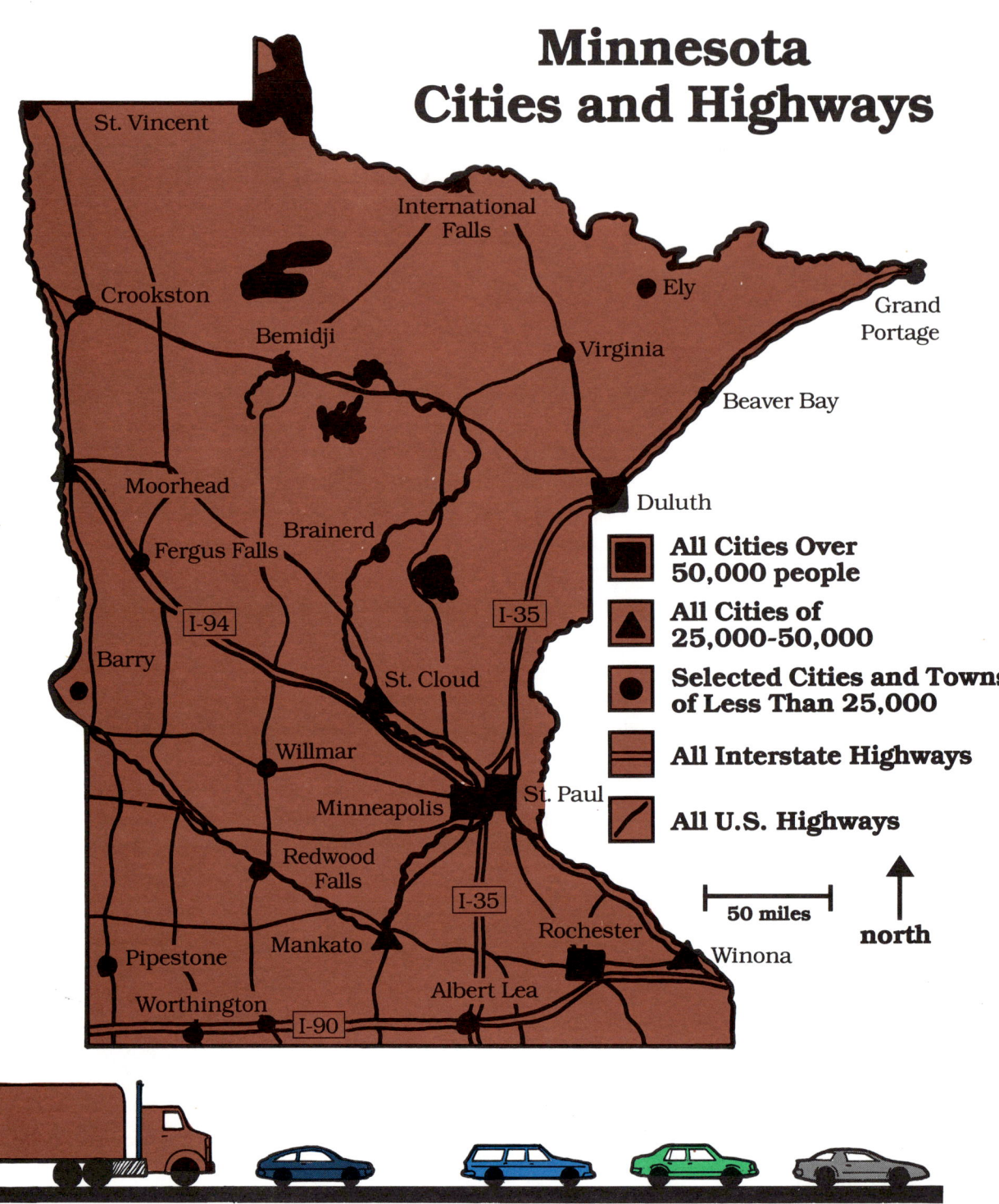

Chapter 9

People, Cities, and Highways

Minnesota has slightly more than four million people. These people have built cities and towns, highways, farms, and mines. They have developed parks, forests, and trails. The ancestors of most Minnesotans came from Europe; a few are Native Americans.

Sioux and Chippewa Indians lived in Minnesota before 1500. By the early 1600s French explorers and fur traders had entered the region. When Fort Snelling was built in 1819, white settlers began to move into the state from New York and New England. A railroad connecting St. Paul to the East Coast, completed in 1867, brought the first large group of European settlers to Minnesota.

Germans and Norwegians, the state's largest immigrant groups, settled in southern Minnesota during the late 1880s. Slightly later Southern and Eastern Europeans settled in the Twin Cities and on the Mesabi Iron Range. Blacks came from the American South during the mid-1900s. Mexican Americans, East Asians, Southeast Asians, and Cubans have more recently joined Minnesota's ethnic mix.

These people have built more than 1,000 cities and towns interconnected by approximately 130,000 miles of highways and roads. This is more miles of road than in any other state except Kansas, California, Illinois, and Texas.

Minnesota's five largest cities (1988 census) are Minneapolis with 355,800 people, St. Paul with 265,100, Bloomington with 85,299, Duluth with 82,899, and Rochester with 64,797. The Twin Cities metropolitan area — Minneapolis, St. Paul, and surrounding suburbs — has more than two million people, half the state's population.

Some of Minnesota's smallest towns include Beaver Bay with a population of 218 people, St. Vincent with a population of 143, and Barry with a population of 43.

Minnesota's highway system is dominated by Interstates 35, 90, and 94. Federal, state, and county highways run between them. Interstates 90 and 94 run east-west across northern United States, connecting Minnesota with both the Atlantic and Pacific coasts. Interstate 35, running north-south through central United States, connects Minnesota with Mexico. Minnesotans and their settlements, once isolated from one another by long oxcart trails and winding streams, are now closely tied to the rest of the nation and world.

wilderness scene — BWCAW

urban scene — St. Paul

Minnesota's population density, persons/square mile, ranges from ≤ 5 in the northeast to ≥ 2,000 in the Twin Cities

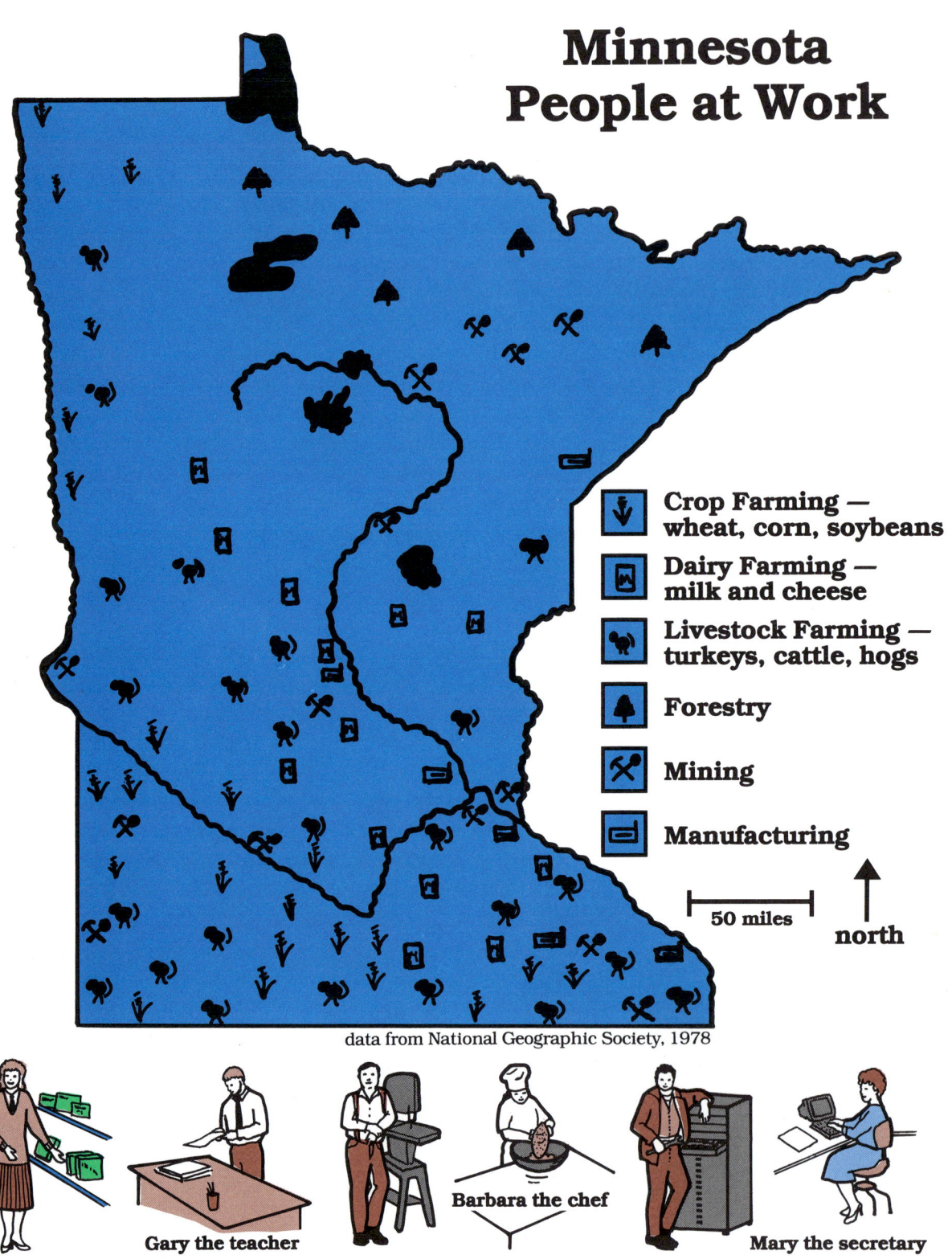

Chapter 10

People at Work

Minnesotans, blessed with a moist variable climate, rich soils, moderate topography, substantial mineral wealth, central location, and excellent transportation routes, work at a wide variety of occupations.

Approximately 34 percent of Minnesotans live in the country. Most of these people work at farming, forestry, and mining. Approximately 66 percent of Minnesotans live in towns and cities. Most of these people work in manufacturing, trade, finance, banking and insurance, transportation, and tourism.

Minnesota farmers are among the most productive in the world. They grow wheat, corn, and soybeans; grass, clover, and flax seed; oats, sunflowers, sugar beets, rye, barley, hay, peas, and Christmas trees. They raise cattle, turkeys, hogs, and mink. They produce milk, butter, cheese, and eggs. In 1987 Minnesota had 85,079 farms, covering approximately 27 million acres.

Minnesota foresters cut trees for lumber, paper, posts, railroad ties, fuel, and other products. Minnesota miners extract iron ore, gravel, sand, clay, peat, and stone. They use these materials in the production of steel, fertilizer, roads, glass, fuel, potting soil, pipes, tiles, and buildings.

More Minnesotans work in sales than in any other business. In 1988 over 506,000 people worked at buying and selling just about everything from toothpicks to barges. Manufacturing, however, is Minnesota's greatest money-making business. In 1985 it generated close to 20 billion dollars. Minnesotans manufacture computers and other electronic equipment, non-electrical machinery, metal products, paper products, chemicals, and industrial instruments.

Minnesotans working in finance, banking, and insurance make the Twin Cities the financial center of the Upper Midwest. Other Minnesotans move people and materials into, away from, and around the state. They work with trucks, buses, trains, planes, ships, pipelines, and power lines. Still other Minnesotans work in tourism helping millions of travelers each year, in education giving the state one of the best school systems in the country, and in health care making Minneapolis and Rochester world-renowned. They also work in social services, legal services, construction, and government.

farmer feeding her calf

man repairing power lines

physician examining a patient

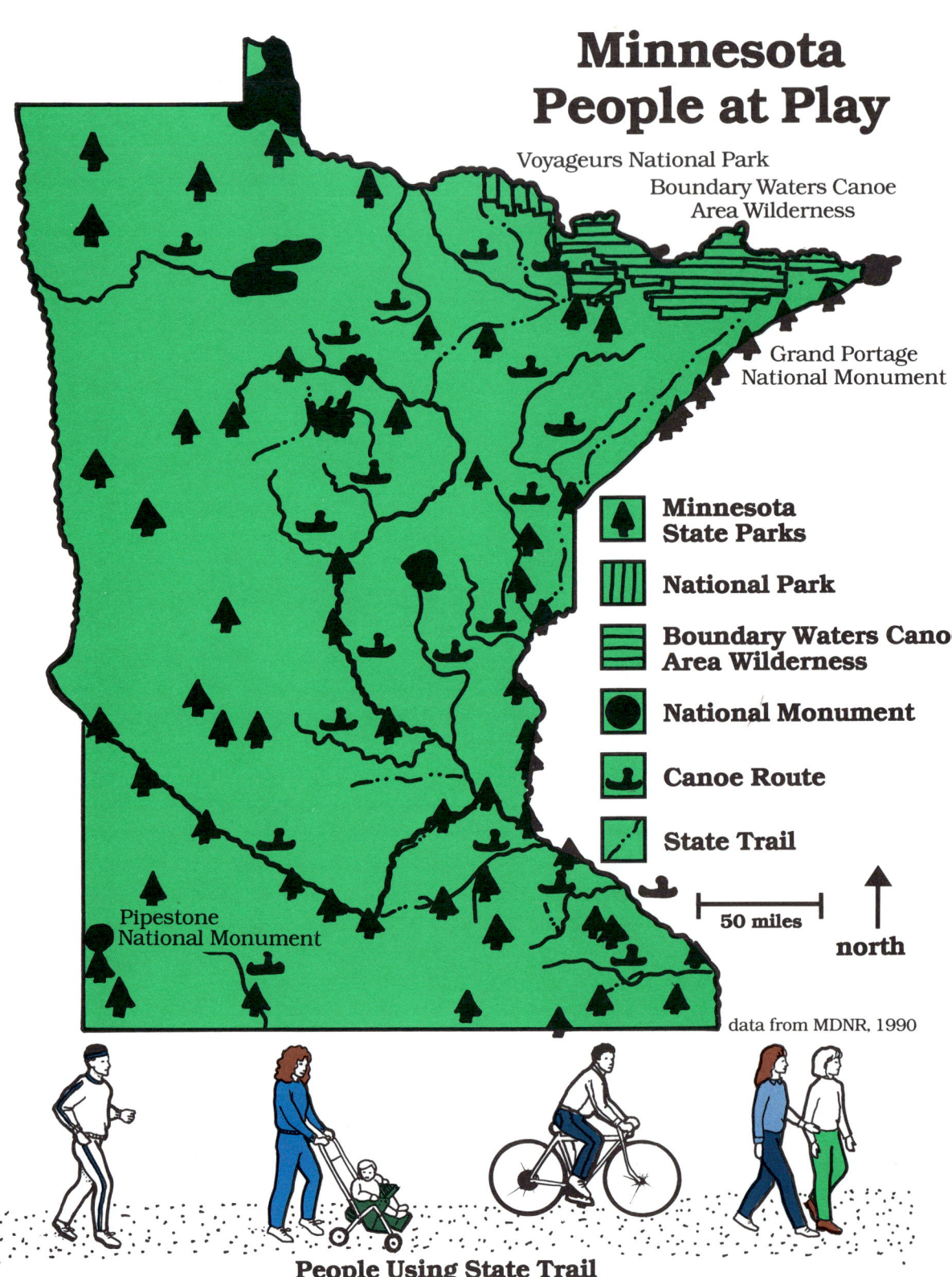

Chapter 11

People at Play

Minnesotans love the outdoors. They enjoy their many lakes and rivers, changing weather, diverse vegetation, and varying landscapes. During the summer they canoe, swim, sail, waterski, and bicycle. They play soccer, baseball, golf, and tennis. In the winter they ski, skate, dog-sled, slide, play hockey, and build snow sculptures. Minnesotans like football in the autumn, baseball and kite-flying in the spring. They camp, fish, hike, and hunt throughout the year.

Minnesotans have set aside much land and water for these activities. The state owns more land than any other except Alaska. Minnesota's 64 state parks cover more than 171,000 acres; Voyageurs National Park covers another 219,000 acres. These parks provide camping areas, picnic grounds, swimming beaches, boat landings, and hiking trials. Approximately seven million people visit them each year.

Minnesota's 55 state and two national forests cover more than three million acres and provide camping, hiking, fishing, and other recreational opportunities. The Boundary Waters Canoe Area Wilderness, part of Superior National Forest and the only federally protected canoe wilderness in the country, includes more than a thousand lakes and many thousands of islands. It has 1,200 canoe routes and more than 2,000 designated campsites.

Minnesota has two national monuments — Grand Portage and Pipestone. It also has thousands of city, county, and regional parks; school and city athletic fields; tennis courts, golf courses, swimming pools, private resorts, campgrounds, water accesses, and marinas.

The state's public trails provide space for snowmobiling, horseback and bicycle riding, cross-country skiing, hiking, backpacking, and jogging. Minnesota's snowmobile trails run for nearly a thousand miles, a greater distance than those of any other state. Its 11 multi-use trails run for more than 1,200 miles.

Boating, fishing, and hunting are three of Minnesota's most popular sports. People come from all over the world to participate in them. The state has 2.6 million acres of boating waters in lakes more than 50 acres in size, 18 "Canoe and Boating Rivers" running 2,208 miles, and 11 million acres of public hunting land. There are approximately two million licensed anglers in the state and 600,000 hunters.

sailing　　　　cross-country skiing　　　　camping

Minnesota — More Maps

Map A

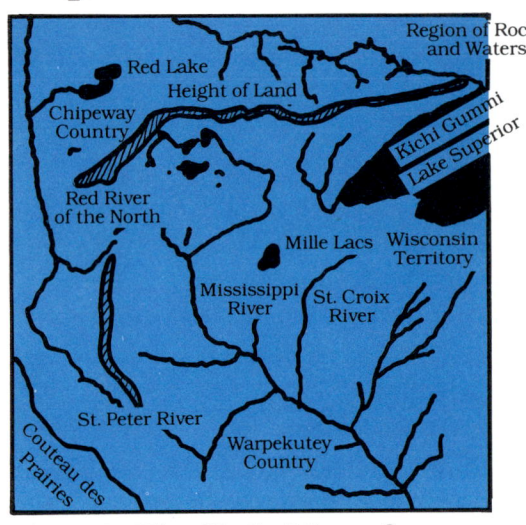

J. Nicollet's Map of Minnesota Territory 1843
— greatly simplified and reduced

Map B

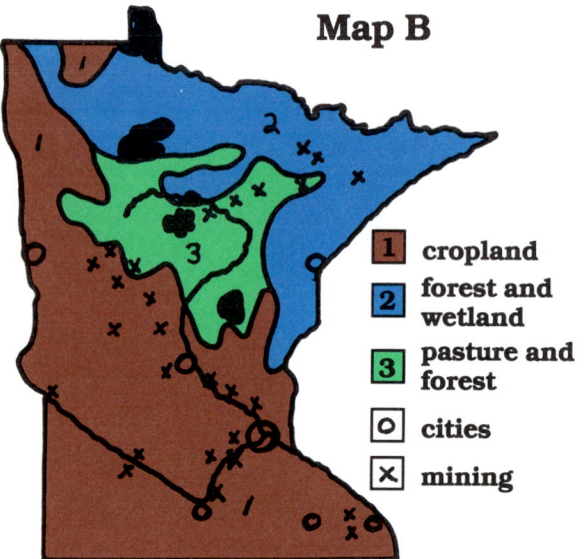

1. cropland
2. forest and wetland
3. pasture and forest
- cities
- mining

simplified from Borchert & Yaeger, 1968

Minnesota Land Use

Map C

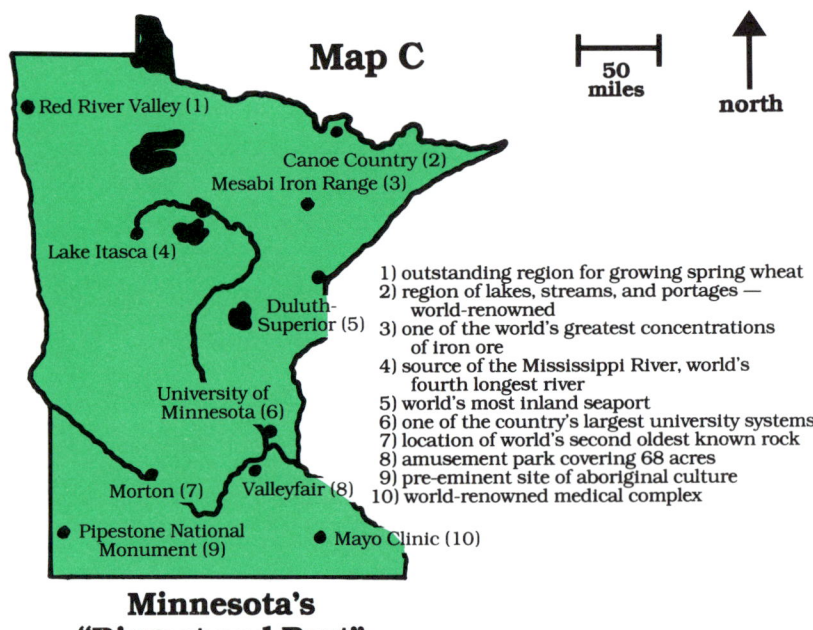

1) outstanding region for growing spring wheat
2) region of lakes, streams, and portages — world-renowned
3) one of the world's greatest concentrations of iron ore
4) source of the Mississippi River, world's fourth longest river
5) world's most inland seaport
6) one of the country's largest university systems
7) location of world's second oldest known rock
8) amusement park covering 68 acres
9) pre-eminent site of aboriginal culture
10) world-renowned medical complex

Minnesota's "Biggest and Best"

Chapter 12

More Maps

You have seen maps of lakes and rivers, hills and plains, climate, plants, cities, highways, and parks. You have seen maps at varying scales. For example, on page 4, one inch on the map is equal to approximately 2,000 miles on the ground. On pages 6, 8, and 10, one inch equals approximately 62 miles. There are, of course, many other kinds of maps and many other map scales. Map content depends on the information people are looking for. Map scale depends on the information people have and the detail they need.

Map A, on the facing page, is Joseph N. Nicollet's map of what is now Minnesota. Nicoliet, a Frenchman, explored and mapped the Upper Mississippi River Basin during the years 1836-1840. Map B shows the present-day land use of the state. Minnesotans use almost half, 44%, of their state for growing crops and slightly more than one-third, 34%, for forest. They use 11% for pasture, 2% for cities, towns, and highways, and 0.1% for mining. The remaining 9% of the state is covered by lakes, rivers, and wetlands. Map C indicates the location of some of the state's "Biggest and Best."

Map D, below, is an enlargement of Minneapolis-St. Paul. It has a scale of one inch to approximately 20 miles. Notice that these cities are located at the intersection of the Mississippi and Minnesota rivers. Here, alongside two major trade routes, the early settlers found abundant water power, rich soils, and heavy timber. Map E is an enlargement of Duluth-Superior and its harbor, the protected mouth of the St. Louis River. Duluth-Superior is the world's most inland seaport. Minnesotans ship and receive iron ore, grain, cement, and many other bulk goods directly to and from countries throughout the world.

Go now with all that you have learned of maps and of Minnesota. Go with all that you have learned of how the varying natural features of a particular area relate to one another and tie into the life of its peoples. You may read about, travel to, and perhaps live in other regions. Relate what you have learned here to the rest of the world around you.

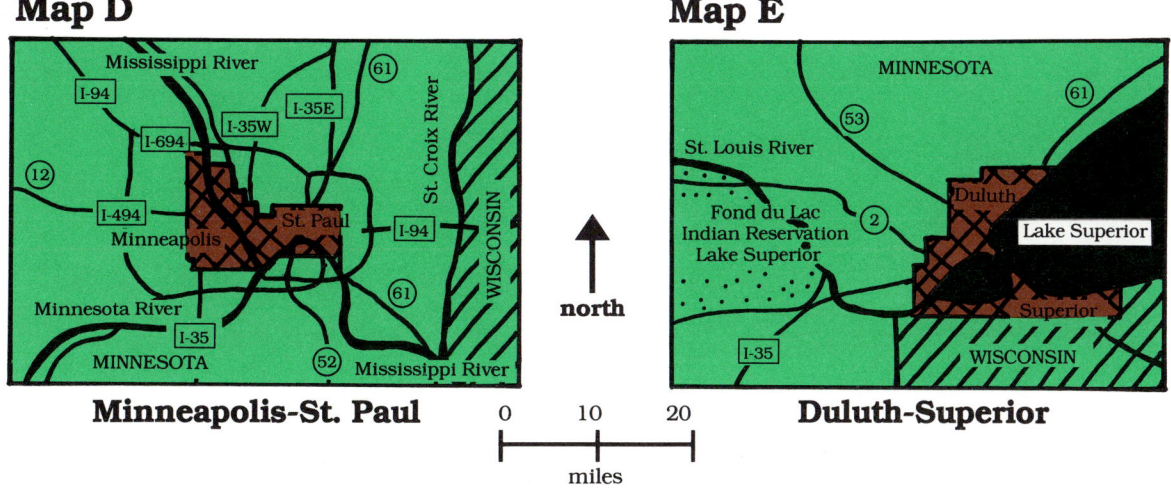

If You Want to Know More:

Cited References

Borchert and Gustafson. 1980. *Atlas of Minnesota Resources and Settlement.* University of Minnesota and the Minnesota State Planning Agency.

Borchert and Yaeger. 1968. *Atlas of Minnesota Resources and Settlement.* Minnesota State Planning Agency.

Espenshade, E., ed. 1990. *Goode's World Atlas 18th Edition.* Rand McNally.

Grigal, D., ed. 1983. *Suborders of Minnesota Soils* (map) in Anderson and Grigal. 1984. "Soils and Landscapes of Minnesota." Minnesota Agricultural Extension Service.

Grossman and Thomsen, eds. 1987. *The Minnesota Almanac 1988.* John L. Brekke and Sons.

Küchler, A. *Natural Vegetation* (map) in Espenshade, 1990.

Marshner, F. 1930. *The Original Vegetation of Minnesota* (map). North Central Forest Experiment Station.

Minnesota Department of Natural Resources. 1990.

Morey, G. 1976. *Geological Map of Minnesota: Bedrock Geology.* Minnesota Geological Survey.

National Geographic Society. 1978. *National Geographic Picture Atlas of Our Fifty States.*

Watson and Gilbert. 1989. *Minnesota Weatherguide 1990 Calendar.* Freshwater Foundation, WCCO Weather Center, The Science Museum of Minnesota.

Wright, H. "Physiography of Minnesota" in Sims and Morey, eds. 1972. *Geology of Minnesota: A Centennial Volume.* Minnesota Geological Survey.

Suggestions for Further Reading

Broekel, R. 1983. *Maps and Globes.* Childrens Press.

Federal Writers' Project of the Works Progress Administration. *The WPA Guide to Minnesota.* Minnesota Historical Society Press. 1985.

Gilbert, J. 1983. *Jim Gilbert's Nature Notebook.* Minnesota Landscape Arboretum.

Hazard, E. 1982. *The Mammals of Minnesota.* University of Minnesota Press.

Janssen, R. 1987. *Birds in Minnesota.* University of Minnesota Press.

Johnson, P. 1987. *Minnesota: Portrait of the Land and its People.* American Geographic Publishing.

Minnesota Department of Natural Resources. 1989. *. . . the Uncommon Ones: Minnesota's Endangered Plants and Animals.*

Minnesota Department of Natural Resources. no date. *Trees of Minnesota.*

Minnesota Department of Transportation. *Official Highway Map of Minnesota 1989-1990.* St. Paul.

Moyle and Moyle. 1977. *Northland Wild Flowers.* University of Minnesota Press.

Sansome, C. 1983. *Minnesota Underfoot: A Field Guide to the State's Outstanding Geologic Features.* Voyageur Press.

Umhoefer, J. 1984. *Guide to Minnesota's Parks, Canoe Routes and Trails.* Northword.

Waters, T. 1977. *The Streams and Rivers of Minnesota.* University of Minnesota Press.

Places to Visit

The Depot, 506 West Michigan Street, Duluth. The restored Duluth train depot features an old steam train, numerous historic photographs, and the St. Louis County Heritage and Arts Center.

Iron World U.S.A., Highway 169, Box 392, Chisholm. This interpretative center perched on the edge of the Glen Mine portrays the geologic and human history of the Minnesota iron ranges.

James Ford Bell Museum of Natural History, University of Minnesota, 10 Church Street S.E., Minneapolis. This museum is well-known for its dioramas.

Minnesota Landscape Arboretum, 3675 Arboretum Drive, Chanhassen. The Arboretum, lying in an area of hills and wetlands, features extensive areas of wild and cultivated plants.

Science Museum of Minnesota, 30 East 10th Street, St. Paul. Be sure to visit their exhibit, "Our Minnesota: Changing Landscapes."

If You Want to Know More: (continued)

Activities and Questions

(1) Water is one of the world's most valuable natural resources. What exactly is water? Where does it come from? How does it move through the environment? Minnesota has an abundance of both surface and groundwater. Why? How do Minnesotans use their water? What problems face them in their water usage? How are they trying to solve these problems?

(2) Carefully observe the weather, trees, and birds around your home, neighborhood, or school. Identify as many different kinds as possible. Notice how they change over time. Consider keeping a weather log, making a leaf collection, or starting an animal checklist. Travel to another area and observe its weather, trees, and birds. How are they different from those near your home? How are they similar? Why do these differences and similarities exist?

(3) Find out about the early history of your area. When did the first white settlers come to your region? Who lived there before them? Where did both these people come from? Why did they come here? How did they get here? What natural resources, if any, drew them to and kept them in the area? At what did they work?

(4) Look at the means and routes of transportation in your hometown? Where do the people live, work, shop, and vacation? How do they get to and from these places? Have any of these means and routes of transportation changed in the recent past? Do you expect any of them to change in the near future? Why?

(5) Visit a state park. Notice the water, topography, and soils. Describe them. How do these features affect the plant life of the area? How does the plant life affect the animal life? What other natural or man-made attributes of the park affect the plant and animal life? Why have people chosen to make this area a state park?

(6) Examine the area around your home — your yard, neighborhood, and town. How have people changed the shape of the land, the movement of water, the soils, the plant life, the animal life? Why did they do this? Do you think they made any mistakes? Why?

(7) Draw a simple map of your yard, neighborhood, school, or town. Put on the essentials of any good map — title, author, location, direction, legend, date, and scale. Why did you choose to map what you did? What kinds of things did you choose not to map? Why? Of what use is your map?

(8) Contact the Minnesota Department of Natural Resources, the Minnesota Department of Economic Development, and the Minnesota Department of Transportation. What do these agencies do? What are some of Minnesota's other state agencies? Find out about The Nature Conservancy, Audubon Society, and Sierra Club. Gather materials on the Minnesota Natural Heritage Program, the Minnesota Native Plant Society, and the Minnesota Historical Society. What do these organizations do? Consider joining one of them.

Miscellaneous Facts and Figures

Size: 84,088 square miles — 79,289 land; 4,779 water.
Highest Point: Eagle Mountain — 2,301 feet above sea level.
Lowest Point: Lake Superior — 602 feet above sea level.
Majors Rivers: Mississippi, Minnesota, St. Croix, Red, Rainy.
Drainage Directions: north to Hudson Bay, east to the Gulf of St. Lawrence, south to the Gulf of Mexico.
Number of Lakes: 15,291 covering ten acres or more.
Largest Lake: Red Lake.
Deepest Natural Lake: Lake Saganaga, 240 feet deep.
Average Annual Temperature: 41° F.
Highest Recorded Temperature: 114° F. Beardsley, 1944.
Lowest Recorded Temperature: —59° F. Leech Lake, 1899.
Average Annual Precipitation: 25″.
Greatest Annual Precipitation: 51.5″ Grand Meadow, 1911.
Least Annual Precipitation: 7.8″ Angus, 1936.
Most Rainfall in 24 Hours: 10″ Minneapolis, 1987.
Most Snowfall in 24 Hours: 28″ Grand Portage, 1933.
Largest Hailstone: 5# west central Minnesota, 1910.
Deadliest Tornado: St. Cloud, 1886, killed 74 people.
Number of Native Tree and Shrub Species: approximately 260.
Number of Mammal Species: 80.
Number of Nesting Bird Species: 220.
Population: 4,306,550 people.
Largest City: Minneapolis.
State Capital: St. Paul.
Average Population Density: 50.5 persons per square mile.
Admission to the Union: May 1858.
State Nickname: The North Star State.
State Tree: red (Norway) pine.
State Bird: common loon.
State Flower: showy ladyslipper.
State Rock: Lake Superior agate.

Glossary

These definitions are simplified and pertain only to the word's use in this text. Consult any reliable dictionary for complete definitions.

atlas — a book of maps.
basalt — a dark-colored, fine-grained igneous rock.
billion — a thousand millions, 1,000,000,000.
cicada — a winged insect which emits a loud hum on hot summer days.
clay — a soft plastic earth with extremely small particles.
climate — weather averaged over a long period of time.
conifer — any cone-bearing tree, e.g. a pine or spruce.
deciduous — a tree which loses its leaves in winter, e.g. an oak or maple.
evergreen — any tree that retains its leaves (or needles) throughout the year, e.g. a spruce or palm.
fault — a plane along which rocks have broken and moved.
Fort Snelling — an army post overlooking the confluence of the Mississippi and Minnesota rivers.
fossil — any remains or trace of past life.
geologist — a scientist who studies the earth.
glacier — a moving mass of ice.
gneiss — a banded metamorphic rock.
granite — a common coarse-grained igneous rock composed of both light- and dark-colored minerals.
hardwood — trees with broad flat leaves, such as oak and maple, and usually heavy, compact wood.
igneous rock — a rock formed from the cooling of molten rock material, e.g. granite and basalt.
iron-ore — a rock containing iron.
lake — any standing body of inland water.
landscape — the sum of the scenery, including particularly contour of the land and vegetation.
limestone — a sedimentary rock composed of calcium carbonate.
map — a two-dimensional representation of the earth's surface. A good map must have a title, location, legend, date, author, scale, and orientation.
map scale — the ratio between two points shown on a map and the actual distance between those same two points on the ground.
metamorphic rock — a rock changed from other rocks by high heat and pressure, e.g. gneiss.
millipede — a small many-legged, segmented bug.
mineral — a naturally occurring inorganic substance with a definite range of chemical composition and usually a characteristic crystal form.
organic — composed of decaying plant and animal material.
plain — an extent of level country.
prairie — a large area of level or rolling grass-covered land.
quartz — an extremely common mineral, composed of SiO_2.
relief — the difference in elevation between the high and low points of a land surface.
river — a natural body of flowing water, generally larger than a stream.
rock — a naturally occurring aggregate of minerals.
sandstone — a sedimentary rock composed of sand particles.
sedimentary rock — a rock formed on the surface of the earth from fragments of other rocks, the remains of plants and animals, or chemical precipitates, e.g. limestone and shale.
shale — a sedimentary rock composed of clay particles.
silt — fine-grained rock material, with grains halfway in size between those of sand and clay.
soil — the loose surface of the earth which supports plants.
species — a distinct kind of plant or animal capable of reproducing itself.
topography — the shape or contour of the land.
trailblazer — one who blazes a trail; a leader in any field; a guide.
Trailblazer Books — an independent publisher dedicated to giving people a sense of geographic place; a line of books helping children and adults explore, appreciate, and understand Minnesota's natural heritage.
weather — the condition of the atmosphere with regard especially to moisture, temperature, and wind.
wetland — any lowland area saturated with moisture, e.g. a swamp (tree-covered), marsh (grass and reed-covered), or bog (moss-covered).

Index

Bold numbers refer to pages with illustrations. In a few instances ordering of citations is not strictly alphabetical, but is rather more sensible, e.g., "lakes" precedes "Lake Itasca."

A
Agassiz Lake Plain **8**, **9**
agriculture (see also crops, farms) 9, **22**, 26
animals
    general discussion 10
    illustrations **17**, **18**, **19**, **23**
    miscellaneous 5, 7, 13, 15, 22
Anoka Sandplain **8**

B
Boundary Waters Canoe Area Wilderness 21, **24**, **25**

C
Canada 5, 6, 10, 15
canoe country 26
canoeing rivers **24**, 25
central Minnesota **8**, **9**, 11, 15
cities and towns
    general discussion 21
    illustrations **20**, **21**, **26**
    land use 9, 23, 26, 27
    statistics 4
climate 5, **12**, **13**, 15, 25
crops 5, 15, **22**, 23, 26, 27
cross-sections 7, **8**, 14

D
drainage basins **6**, 7
Duluth, Duluth-Superior **20**, 26, 27

E
Eagle Mountain **8**, 9
Earth (see world)

F
facts, figures, comparisons 4, 6, 26, 29
farms, farming, farmlands 5, **15**, **18**, 21, **22**, 23
faults **10**, 11
Fond du Lac Indian Reservation 27
forest
    general discussion 17
    illustrations 7, **16**, **24**, **26**
    miscellaneous 5, 15, 18, 25, 27
forestry **22**, 23
fossils **10**, 11

G
geologic time 10
geologist 11
Giant's Range **8**
glaciers, glaciation 5, 9, 15
Glacial Lake Agassiz (see also Agassiz Lake Plain) 9
glacial plains **8**
Grand Portage National Monument 24

H
highways 9, **20**, 21, 27
hills 5, **8**, 9
Hudson Bay **4**, 5

Great Lakes 7
Gulf of Mexico **4**, 5, 7
Gulf of St. Lawrence **4**, 7

I
Indian heritage 7, **26**, 27
iron ore 5, **10**, 11
iron ranges **10**, 11

J, K, L
lakes
    general discussion 5, 7
    illustrations **6**, **7**
    statistics 6
    miscellaneous 19, 26, 27
Lake Itasca **6**, 26
Lake Mille Lacs **6**, 26
Lake Superior 5, 6, 7, **8**, 9, **17**, **26**, 27
land use 9, **26**, 27
landscapes 5, **8**, **9**, **14**, 21
Leaf Hills **8**, 9

M
maps, general, definition and scale 27
maps, Minnesota
    animal life **18**, **19**
    climate **12**, **13**
    hills, plains, and valleys **8**
    lakes, rivers, and streams **6**
    outline **frontispiece**, 4
    people at play **24**
    people at work **22**
    people, cities, and highways **20**
    plant life **16**
    rocks **10**
    soils **14**
    miscellaneous 26, 27
maps, world **4**, **5**, **12**
maps, miscellaneous 16, 27
Mayo Clinic 26
medicine 23, 26
Mesabi Iron Range 21, 26
minerals 11, 23
mining **22**, 26, 27
Minneapolis **20**, **21**, 27
Minneapolis-St. Paul 4, 21, 23, **27**
Minnesota
    overview 4
    statistics and facts 4, 5, 6, 21, 29

Minnesota River **6,** 7, **27**
Minnesota River Valley **8, 11**
Minnesota Territory **26, 27**
Misquah Hills 9
Mississippi River **4,** 5, **6,** 7, **26, 27**
Mississippi River Valley 8
Morton **10,** 11, **26**
Morton Gneiss **10,** 11, **26**
mountains **4, 8, 9,** 11

N
national forests, monuments, parks **24,** 25
natural resources, use and modification
  7, 9, 11, 13, 15, 17, 19, 26
Nicollet, Joseph **26,** 27
North Shore 7, 11
northern Minnesota 11
northeastern Minnesota **8, 9,** 15, 17, 18
northwestern Minnesota 9

O
oceans **4, 5,** 7
occupations (see work)
ores **10,** 11

P
parks **24, 25, 26**
people
  general discussion 5, 21, 23, 25
  illustrations **7, 20, 22, 23, 24, 25, 26, 27**
  statistics 21, 23
  use and modification of natural resources
    7, 9, 11, 13, 15, 17, 19, 26
Pipestone National Monument **24, 26**
plains **8, 9**
plants
  general discussion 17
  illustrations **16**
  miscellaneous 5, 7, 15, 19
play (see recreation)
population **4, 20,** 21
prairie 5, 15, **16,** 17, 18
precipitation 4, 13

Q, R
rivers and streams
  general discussion 7
  illustrations **4, 5, 6, 7, 26**
  statistics 6
  miscellaneous 18, 21, 27
recreation 5, **7,** 9, **13,** 18, **24, 25**
Red Lake **6,** 7, **26**
Red River of the North **6,** 7, **26**
Red River Valley **9, 26**
river basins **6**
Rochester **20,** 23
rocks
  general discussion 5, 11
  illustrations **8, 10**
  miscellaneous 15, **26**

S
St. Croix River **6,** 7, **26,** 27
St. Croix River Valley 8
St. Louis River **6,** 7, **27**
St. Paul **20, 21, 27**
Sawtooth Mountains **8, 9**
seasons **5, 13,** 25
Smoky Hills **8**
snow **13,** 29
soils 5, **14, 15, 23**
southern Minnesota 15, 17, 19, 21
southeastern Minnesota 9, 17
southwestern Minnesota 9
sports (see recreation)
state forests, parks, and trails **24,** 25
storms 13, 29
swamps (see wetlands)

T
temperature 4, 13, 29
topography 4, **8,** 9, 15, 23
trade routes 27
trails 21, **24,** 25
transportation 9, **20,** 21, 23, 27
trees (see also forests) 5, 17

U
University of Minnesota **26**

V
Valleyfair **26**
valleys **8, 9, 11**
vegetation (see also crops, forests, plants)
  16, 17, 25
Vermilion fault **10**
volcanism 11
Voyageurs National Park **24,** 25

W
Wisconsin **6, 26, 27**
water (see also lakes, rivers, wetlands)
  general discussion 7
  illustrations **6, 25, 26, 27**
  statistics **4**
  miscellaneous **5,** 9, 15, 27
weather 13, 25, 29
western Minnesota 11, 17
wetlands 5, 15, **16,** 17, 18, **26,** 27
wilderness **21**
work 5, **15, 22, 23**
world **4, 5, 10,** 12

X, Y, Z

Books may be purchased at your local bookstore, ordered from Voyageur Press, or ordered directly from Trailblazer Books for $12.95 (softcover), $17.95 (hardcover), + 6½% Minnesota sales tax, + $2.00 shipping and handling on all orders.